Collector's Guide To
Country Store Antiques

Don and Carol Raycraft

Collector's Guide To

Country Store Antiques

Don and Carol Raycraft

COLLECTOR BOOKS
A Division of Schroeder Publishing Co., Inc.

The current values in this book should be used only as a guide. They are not intended to set prices, which vary from one section of the country to another. Auction prices as well as dealer prices vary greatly and are affected by condition as well as demand. Neither the Author nor the Publisher assumes responsibility for any losses that might be incurred as a result of consulting this guide.

Printed by IMAGE GRAPHICS, INC., Paducah, Kentucky

Acknowledgments

Arthur Elliott
Mr. & Mrs. Ken Elliott
Lucile Steidinger
Emma Lou Raycraft
Bernice Veatch
Kent Ryan
Joe & Opel Pickens
Bill Schroeder
Steve Quertermous
Edna Faulkner
Ervin & Lois Bergen

Photography

Jon Balke
Carol Raycraft
Bob Farling

Introduction

When I was a child in the 1940's, neighborhood grocery stores were a major focus of my youth. Within a six block radius of my house there were four emporiums that sold Bowmen baseball cards, Double Cola, Black Jack Gum and ice cream cones with the potential for a slip of paper in the bottom that entitled the bearer to a free sample on the next visit.

As a grade school student, the highlight of my day was receiving a nickel from my father on my way out the door each weekday morning. I contemplated through geography, cursive writing practice and language arts precisely what candy bar I was going to purchase over the lunch break at Snyder's Grocery. A Chicken Dinner, Forever Yours or Whiz Bar usually was my final choice.

My friend Craig Bazzani and I were under the impression that every school in each of the forty-eight states had laws that made it mandatory for elementary schools to have a grocery store next door or across the street. The store next to my wife's grade school in southern Illinois was a combination grocery-bait shop.

The high school I attended was within two blocks of another neighborhood grocery run by an elderly man and his wife. The noon hour arrangement in this store was unique because the store offered cold cut sandwiches, Blue Star potato chips and soft drinks in a cooler filled with ice water. The customer ordered slices of bread and meat, made his own sandwiches, kept track of what he ate and then reported to the owner who calculated the bill. In retrospect, I would guess that many of us suffered serious memory lapses between the last bite and the cash register.

Shortly after my wife and I were married, we moved to a small central Illinois community that contained a barber shop, pool hall, bank, restaurant and an unkept building that sold "general merchandise." The business had been in operation since the early 1900's and was managed by the two surviving daughters of the original owner. There are probably similar stores in small towns somewhere in America today but this was our only experience. To walk in the front door was to step back in time and observe a store filled with merchandise that had been carefully put on shelves seventy-five years before in anticipation of a quick sale. The ladies who managed the business took their roles seriously. They appeared to have no concept that the world had passed them by. They were content to conduct themselves each day in much the same fashion as had their father. The people in the farming community thought little about the store. They didn't think it was especially unusual because it had been on the same corner doing business as usual before the majority of them had been born.

We visited the store many times and tried to buy the spool cabinets, coffee bins and advertising signs that covered the walls. We were quietly and firmly told that those things were not for sale.

Only in later years after the sisters had died and the building was closed did we realize the significance of what had been there.

Historical Perspective

The first shopkeepers in New England in the late seventeenth century and throughout the eighteenth century sold products that were locally made or grown. When goods were imported for sale in the colonies few were labeled so brand names were not important.

The first products to carry brand names were medicines, beer, wine and tobacco. The packages were very simply designed because the majority of the consumers could not read. Packaging was developed to protect the product and increase its shelf life rather than to promote its sale. The paper labels were also printed on handpowered wooden presses and the bottles were individually blown.

Most of the products were carried home in cloth or crude paper bags that the customer brought with him to the store. Shopkeepers seldom furnished containers for their goods until the mid-nineteenth century.

After the 1850's national brands began to compete with local products on grocers' shelves. As the literacy rate increased, elaborate and colorful advertisements carrying outrageous claims were produced to sell goods to consumers. By 1900 the glass industry had evolved to the point that an English machine could manufacture more than 1,000 bottles each day.

Country stores in all sections of the nation were gathering places for locals to discuss the problems of the day. This picture was taken near Virginia Beach, Virginia in the 1930's.

The "golden age" of the country store was between 1880 and 1940. Large national grocery chains (A&P) were not yet major competition and local groceries flourished.

After the Civil War the factories of the industrialized North that had initially been created to produce food, supplies and armaments for the war effort, began to manufacture household goods on a large scale. At the same time new areas were being opened and additional states were gradually taking the place of territories.

Country stores took on new importance as the population grew and the public roadways were improved. The stores offered credit, tools, candy, seed, clothing, groceries, a post office and extended debates on a thousand topics.

In the fall, summer and spring the front porches of most stores were crowded with locals solving the problems of the day. The winter months found the conversations adjourned to the chairs surrounding a pot bellied stove in the rear of the stores. The floors in the immediate area of the stoves were littered with boxes of sand that served as inexpensive spittoons. Endless checker games and marathon whittling sessions made the winters pass painlessly for those not inclined to "discussions."

Many country and small town stores contained Masonic Halls or other lodges on the second floor. Entry to the lodge meeting rooms was usually made by an exterior stairway on the side of the building.

This store from the early 1920's would be a collector's dream if it were possible to escape back into time with a twenty dollar bill, thirty minutes and a truck to bring it home.

The sixty years between 1880 and 1940 provided a unique period in the history of the American country store as this was the age of the traveling salesman or "drummer" who journeyed from hamlet to crossroad settlement selling his wares. The arrival of the "drummer" could become a minor celebration in many communities because he brought news from places many locals had only read about. The drummer's suitcases were filled with samples of new products and his arrival was eagerly anticipated. Drummers who represented grocery wholesalers passed through every four to six weeks and tool or seed purveyors at six to eight month intervals.

The early drummers rode in horse drawn carts before the railroads became the primary means of transportation in the late nineteenth century. The national highway system began to develop in the 1930's and many drummers began to use automobiles. The hotels that depended on "traveling men" for much of their business in small towns across America gradually began to close. The demise of the hotels was followed by the individually owned grocery and general stores that were replaced in the 1940's and 1950's by supermarkets and chain stores.

Sparsely furnished store that appears long on staff and short on merchandise. Note the pressed tin ceiling that was typical of midwestern grocery stores in the 1920's.

The Golden Age

The neighborhood grocery in many communities filled food orders, made deliveries and issued extensive credit in the 1880-1940 period. There was little need for advertising because most of the stores purchased their goods in the same limited quantities from wholesalers and the pricing structures were almost identical. Competition was kept at a minimum and most people bought their groceries in the small store near homes.

The store carried meat cut to order, fruits and vegetables, a limited variety of canned goods and cereals without sugar but with secret agent spy scopes or decoder rings.

Oak store fixtures and the extensive use of glass cases make this an attractive store from the 1905-1910 period. The owner offered an impressive array of medicinal products on the right wall and a wide variety of tobacco, candy, groceries and baked good were also available.

As cities grew and suburban areas gradually began to appear, locally owned grocery stores were replaced by national concerns that offered extensive inventories and heated competition through advertising and promotions. In 1916 Piggly Wiggly opened a self-service grocery in Memphis, Tennessee that revolutionized the business world by doing away with credit and home delivery and demanding cash at the end of a checkout line.

The evolution of the corner grocery store from the locally owned "mom and pop" operation into a supermarket with 18,000 different products, refrigeration, frozen peas and prepackaged meat was inevitable.

The final blow occurred in 1937 with the introduction of the shopping cart. Prior to that date wire baskets with swing handles were carried around the store or the owner searched the shelves with a shopping list provided by the customer at the counter. Instant mashed potatoes, meat extender and artificial salt were still a generation away.

This meat shop owner apparently believed in keeping his overhead down by limiting the range of his offerings. His major expense was saw dust to catch the drippings behind the counter and from the meat hanging at right.

This drug store from the late 1920's or early 1930's even had "official" uniforms for its employees.

Building A Collection

In September of 1985 we attended a "flea" market in Springfield, Ohio, that included more than 2,000 "dealers" offering a cross section of the contents of most of the garages, crawl spaces, attics and basements in middle America. Included among the fan belts, radiator caps, door knobs and fly swatters was a huge assortment of tin food containers, metal signs and advertising memorabilia. The adjectives used to describe this five acre collection could include bent, rusty, broken, reproduced, chipped, cracked, scratched and water stained.

This experience and countless similar trips has underscored to us the necessity to be selective and informed. Buyers must choose only examples in as close to pristine condition as possible. Unlike decorated stoneware pottery and New England painted furniture, country store pieces can literally be uncovered anywhere because country stores were everywhere. We have found exceptional examples from Maine to Texas in shops that specialized in carnival glass, at garage and farm sales, flea markets and prestigous antiques shows in New York City.

As the value of country store antique continues to escalate, the problems of repaired, repainted or reproduced pieces will rise equally as quickly. It has become essential that collectors do their homework before writing the check and that there is a great deal to know and there is not a wealth of sources of information.

Country Store Chronology

1798	Papermaking machine invented in France.
1809	Nicholas Appert invents a practical and convenient technique for preserving food in glass bottles.
1819	Sir Edward Parry takes tinplate containers filled with meat and vegetables on an Artic expedition.
1820	Oysters and salmon are being sold packed in glass bottles in grocery stores in New York City.
1826	John Horniman invents a labor saving machine that fills tea bags.
1830	Huntley and Palmer biscuits are sold in tin boxes to English stagecoach passengers.
1856	Gail Borden receives a patent for processing canned milk.
1866	Beer is first sold in glass bottles.
1870's	"Flat" pocket tins filled with "fine cut" tobacco are available on the streets of Chicago.
1880	Machine-made folding boxes for cigarettes are produced.
1885	Paper bags are commonly being used to package purchases in most American stores.
1890's	Tubes filled with tooth paste are being carried home in paper bags.
1899	Campbell Soup may be purchased for 10ᶜ a can.
1901	"Lunchbox" tobacco containers become available to consumers and remain popular into the 1920's.
1906	Food and Drug Administration begins to limit the claims that can be made by makers of non-prescription drugs.
1912	A patent is issued to American Tobacco Company for "Roly Poly" tobacco containers.
1920's-1930	Peanut butter "pails" are found on grocers' shelves in your hometown.
1935	Cone top and flat top beer cans are first introduced.
1937	Introduction of the shopping cart.
1950's	Large supermarkets quickly replace the neighborhood grocery store.

Kitchell's Candy "lunch pail" container, stenciled label, Bloomington, Illinois, c. 1920.

Holloway's Milk Duds, cardboard boxes, c. early 1940's.

Adams Tutti Frutti chewing gum boxes that contained thirty six bars of five pieces.

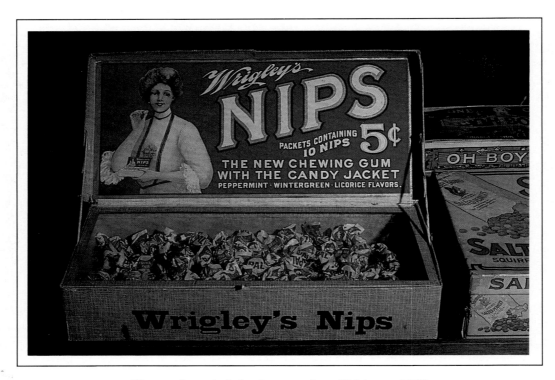

Nips candy coated chewing gum from Wrigley, c. 1940.

Wrigley's gum sign.

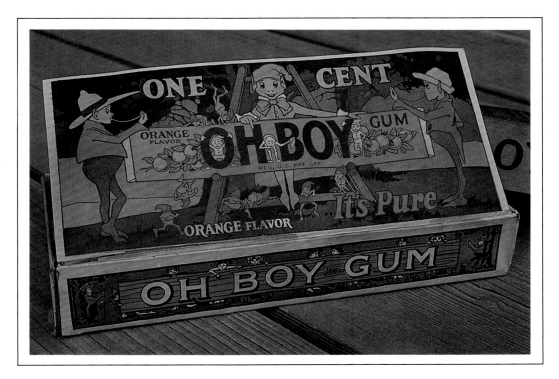

O'Boy Gum box from the 1940's.

Beech-Nut counter display and gum. Individual packages of chewing gum from the 1920-1940 period are difficult to find. Collectors often locate a display rack and then spend years trying to fill it a pack at a time.

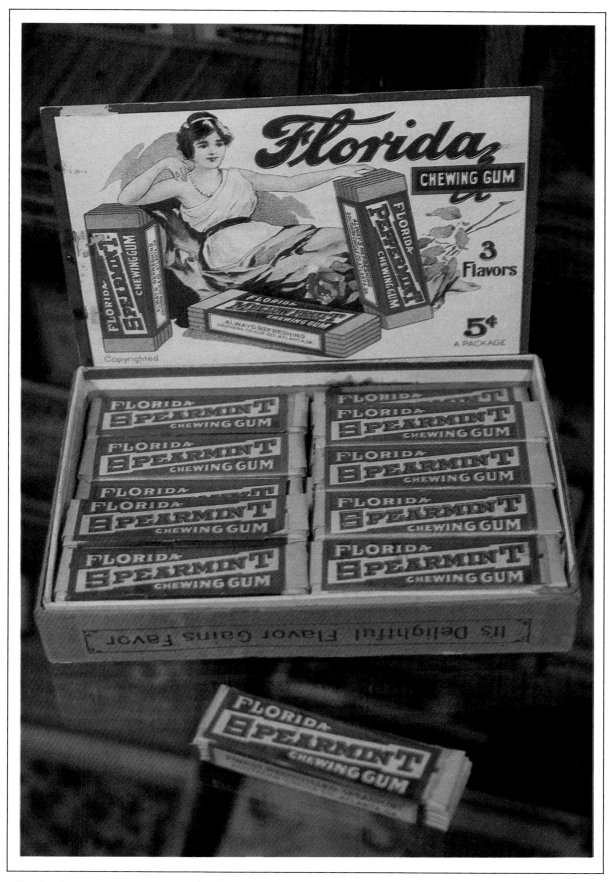

Florida chewing gum, c. 1920's. Florida chewing gum is almost impossible to find in any of its three flavors.

Mavis Mints and El-Peeco Penny Sticks have gone the way of the 25¢ Saturday afternoon at the Esquire Theater with Buster Crabbe and Lash LaRue.

Boxes of Whole Spice.

Durkee and Company spice cannister, early 1900's.

Pepper storage cannister made of cardboard with a wooden top and bottom that was used on store counters.

Stacks of labels originally intended for canned goods periodically come on the market when a warehouse is torn down or the basement of a printer's shop is cleaned out. The salmon labels date from the 1920's and the cans are new.

Relatively few fruit boxes from the 1930's have survived because many were converted into sidewalk racers with the addition of wheels from roller skates. The value of a fruit label is largely determined by the complexity and color of its artwork. It is also difficult to distinguish an old label newly placed on an old box from an original label with its box.

Calumet Baking Powder cans from the 1930's and 1940's.

The Baker's Delight Baking Powder labels are old but the cans they are wrapped around are not. The labels were found in Florida but probably originated on the east coast. They date from the 1920's.

Washington Crisp Corn Flakes.

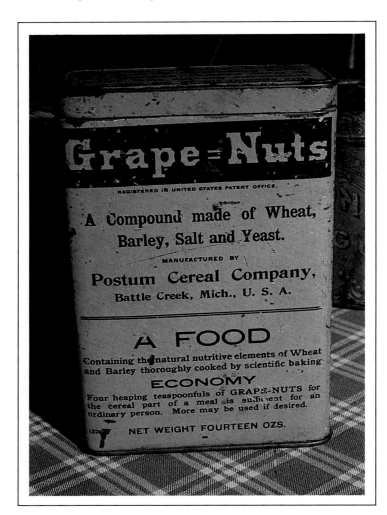

Grape Nuts metal container, c. 1920.

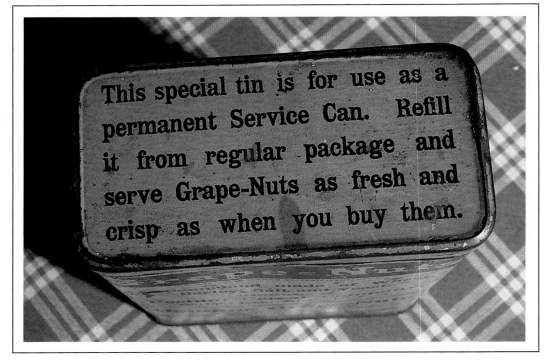

This container was one of the first refillable "boxes."

Bessie's Best Butter boxes, c. 1930's-early 1940's.

Union Grove Milk bottles used for display, c. 1930-1940.

Uncle John's Syrup counter display from the 1920-1930 period.

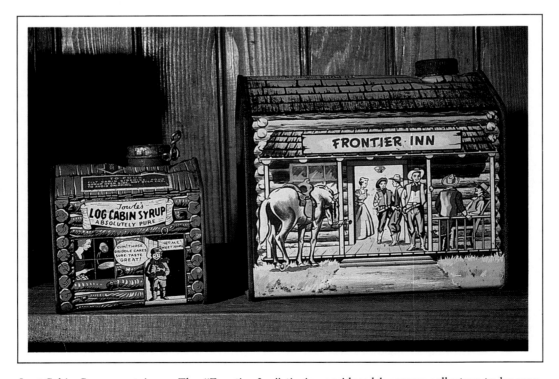

Log Cabin Syrup containers. The "Frontier Inn" tin is considered by many collectors to be rare.

Log Cabin "stand-up" counter display constructed of heavy cardboard with a 1910 copyright. This unusual example measures approximately 28″ x 22″.

Corn Belt Syrup tin with a "drop" or bail handle and a Luxury Coffee container.

Edgemont Cracker and Cake metal overlay and cardboard box for counter display. The grocer kept boxes of crackers on the counter and used a metal overlay with a lift lid for a cover. When the crackers were sold, the box was thrown away and the overlay was used again with another full box.

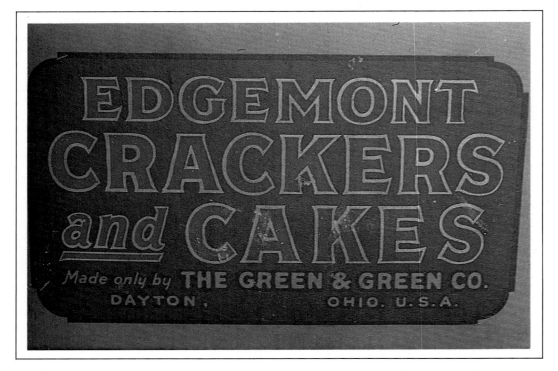

The cardboard boxes are much more difficult to find than the metal overlays because they were not kept around after the crackers were sold. We have seen stacks of overlays for sale but seldom can find labeled boxes.

Starlight Marshmallow box and overlay from the Virgiel Brothers Grocery in Arrowsmith, Illinois.

Counter cheese cutter.

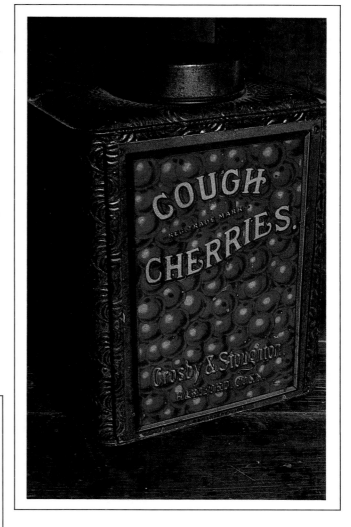

Crosby and Stoughton Cough Cherries, c. 1915.

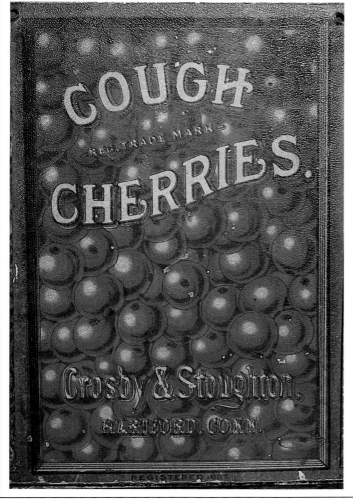

The cough cherry label could be pulled out and another product's logo slipped into the slots on the front of the container.

Tractor Umbrella with unusual advertisements for nonfarm products, c. 1930's. This type of umbrella was sometimes given away with the purchase of a tractor by farm implement dealers. The dealers were provided with the umbrellas by companies who wanted their advertisements to be displayed. Most of the umbrellas were covered with advertisements for farm equipment or seed dealers. Few carried information about "home" or food products.

Grocery bags for small items and penny candy were given to groceries to use while promoting a particular product or service. These date from the first quarter of the twentieth century.

Most grocery stores had cash registers by 1900. The first cash register widely adopted was invented in 1879 by James Ritty (1836-1918) of Dayton, Ohio.

The stores were social centers in rural areas where charity, lottery and basketball tickets were usually available.

Stoneware apple butter jars that could be recycled for home canning. It is almost impossible to find apple butter jars with their original labels. When the jars were repeatedly washed and reused the paper labels gradually were worn away.

Elephant steel wool.

Cardboard sign for Round Oak stoves, ranges and furnaces.

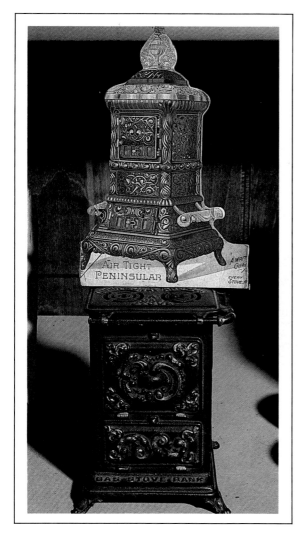

Trade or advertising cards for a stove company. In the 1880-1929 period, trade cards were left at the stores by "drummers" to be given away. For a brief time there was almost a national mania for collecting as many different trade cards as possible. Companies attempted to make their cards as unique and stylish as possible to stimulate sales and interest in their products. Most of the trade cards that were collected were pasted into scrapbooks.

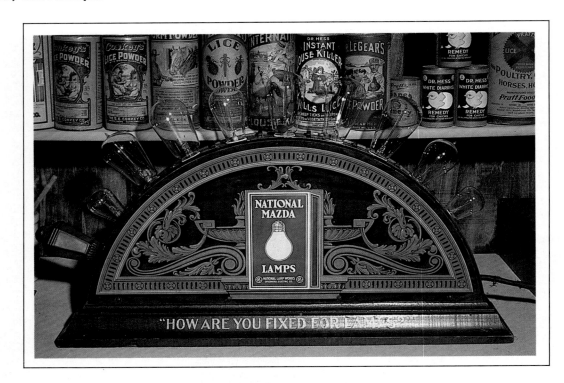

National Mazda counter display for light bulbs, c. 1915.

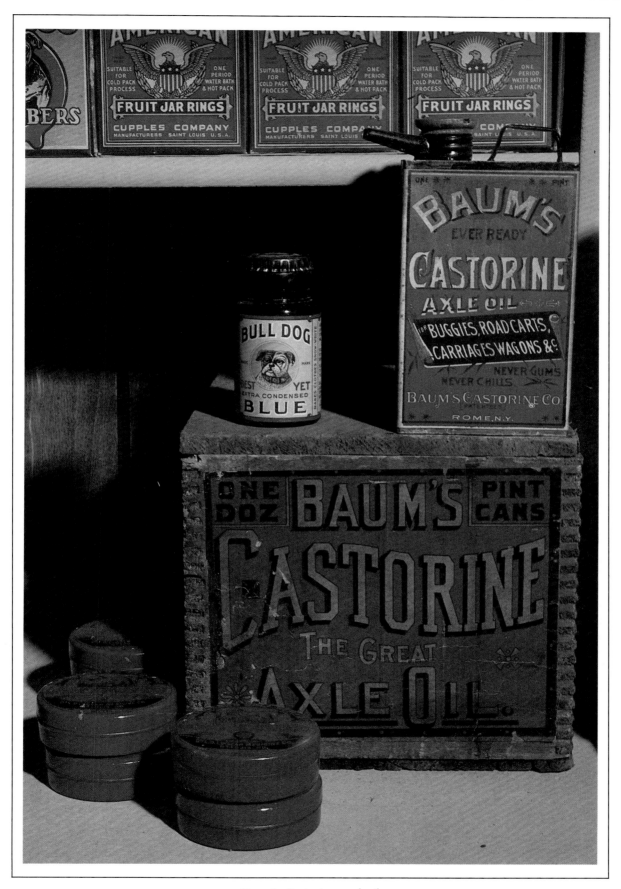

Baum's Castorine axel oil.

Bartlett's Ball Blue box, pine, c. 1900.

Happy Homes Coffee bin, c. 1925. On the "roof" of the bin is a slot for the blend of coffee that the box contains.

Bags for ground coffee, variety of brands, c. 1940.

Jersey Coffee bin, pine, c. early 1900's, stenciled decoration. The value of a wooden or metal coffee bin is significantly diminished if the stenciling or paint has been retouched or restored in any way.

Home Brand and Red Cow coffee tins.

Red Cow coffee in a glass jar.

Ferndell's Coffee tin, three pound size.

Ferndell's coffee grinder for use at home, designed to be nailed to a wall.

DeLeval parts box for cream separators, oak. This case was used to store parts for DeLeval cream separators. Franchised dealers sold and serviced separators for their customers. The parts boxes with the metal front intact and free of rust are difficult to find.

The DeLeval company made four breeds of cows and their calves available to customers as premiums. The eight examples included brown Swiss, Jersey, Guernsey and Holsteins.

Coca-Cola "box" soft drink dispenser, c. 1930's.

Six ounce bottles of Coke were sold for 5¢ with a 2¢ deposit for those who drank while riding their bikes home rather than drinking it in the store.

Squirt grocery sack holder (c. 1940) and Coca-Cola sign from the 1930's.

Huge rolls of waxed wrapping paper from bakeries that have been closed are found occasionally. They have minimal value unless you want to wrap your own bread. Most bread does not have a fifty year shelf life.

Sleepy Eye Flour embossed metal sign, c. 1915. The Massachusetts-based Sleepy Eye Flour Company offered a wide assortment of premiums with the distinctive Indian trademark for their customers. Various sizes of stoneware pitchers that were made for Sleepy Eye at the Monmouth Pottery (Monmouth, Illinois) are eagerly collected today. Metal signs and paper or canvas banners are extremely difficult to find.

Cardboard cylindrical boxes filled with various brands of rolled oats.

Hulman and Company Dauntless Pickles display case, oak and glass, c. 1910.

The Bunny Brand and Hoosier Poet (James Whitcomb Riley) are the most desirable cardboard oats boxes.

Hoosier Poet (James Whitcomb Riley) oats box.

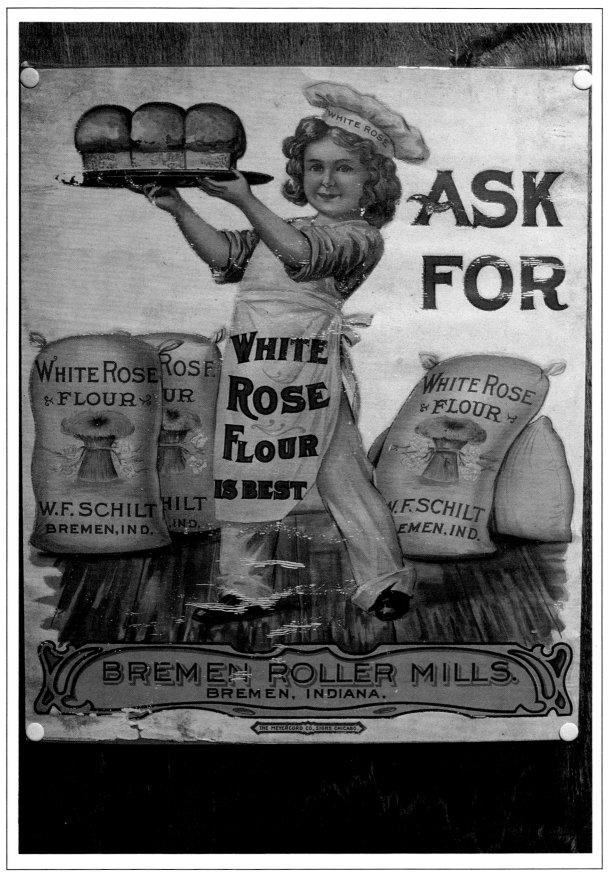

White Rose Flour sign, cardboard.

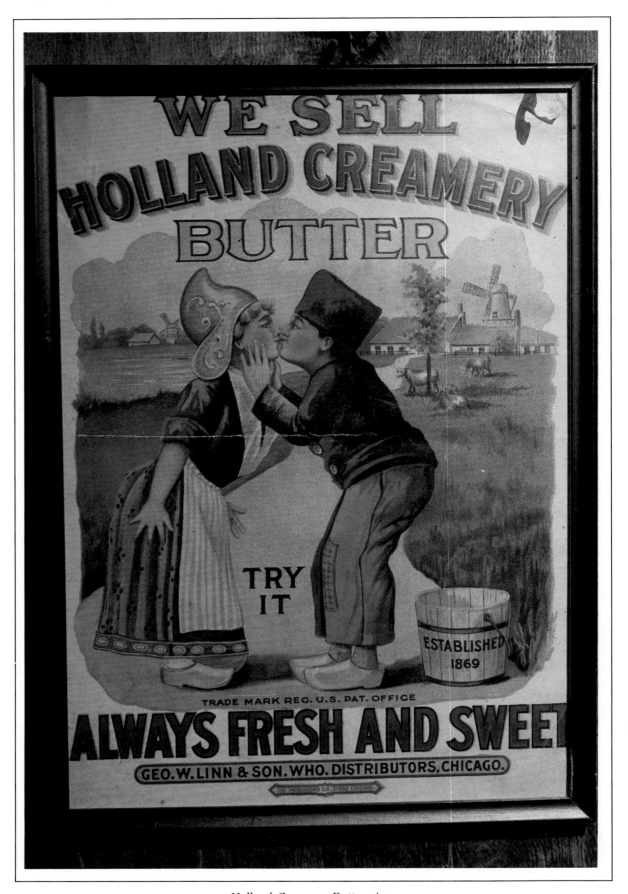

Holland Creamery Butter sign.

Yeast Foam cardboard "stand-up", c. 1920.

Butternut Bread cardboard sign.

Badger and Superior Hops.

Wooden grape containers from the early 1940's.

Unusual oak display counter, c. 1910.

Snow King Baking Powder price board. The "eggs" could be replaced by another item the grocery was trying to sell.

Keystone Mincemeat firkin or bucket, staved construction, pine, bail handle, c. first quarter of the twentieth century.

Golden Drop Plums firkin, c. first quarter of the twentieth century.

Very few firkins can still be found with their original labels.

Apple butter firkin from Schimmel and Company, Philadelphia, c. 1885.

Atmore's Celebrated Mincemeat firkin, c. 1885.

Rolls of Onion Skin toilet paper.

Savory Toilet Paper developed for use in outhouses, c. early 1900's.

Razor blade show case, oak, c. 1890-1910.

Anticor "The Magic Corn Shaver".

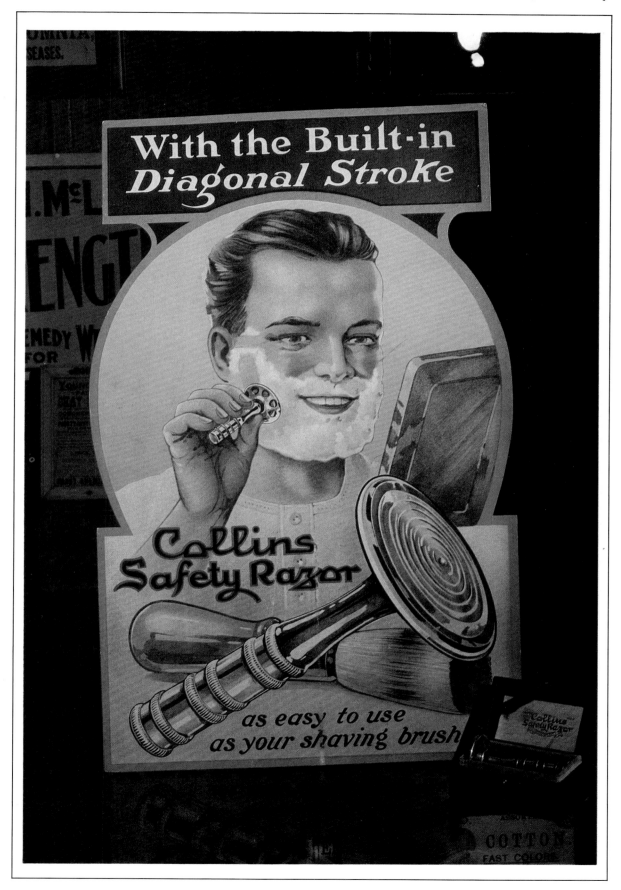

Collins Safety Razor "stand-up" cardboard display, c. 1925.

Shaving brush display case and brushes.

Counter "stand-up" comb display.

Barbours Linen Thread.

Crystal White Family Soap.

Fairbank's Fairy Soap box, pine, colorful interior label.

Fairbank's Gold Dust Washing Powders.

Fun-To-Wash Washing Powders.

Colgate's Octagen Soap boxes.

Old Dutch Cleanser porcelain sign.

Cardboard Old Dutch Cleanser display.

Curved or "half round" Old Dutch Cleanser exterior sign.

Bull Dog Fly and Insect Powder.

K-R-O rat poison "stand-up" cardboard sign.

Bull Dog Jar Rubbers counter display and individual boxes.

Tuf Nut overalls, found in Nebraska, c. 1940, extra large size.

Gold Medal Hosiery counter sign, c. 1920's.

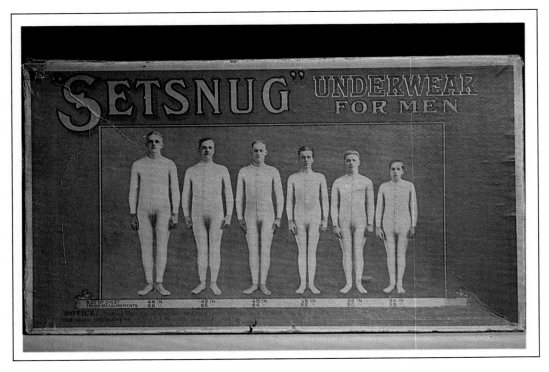

Setsnug Underwear for Men, cardboard box.

Babe Ruth Underwear box,
cardboard, early 1920's.

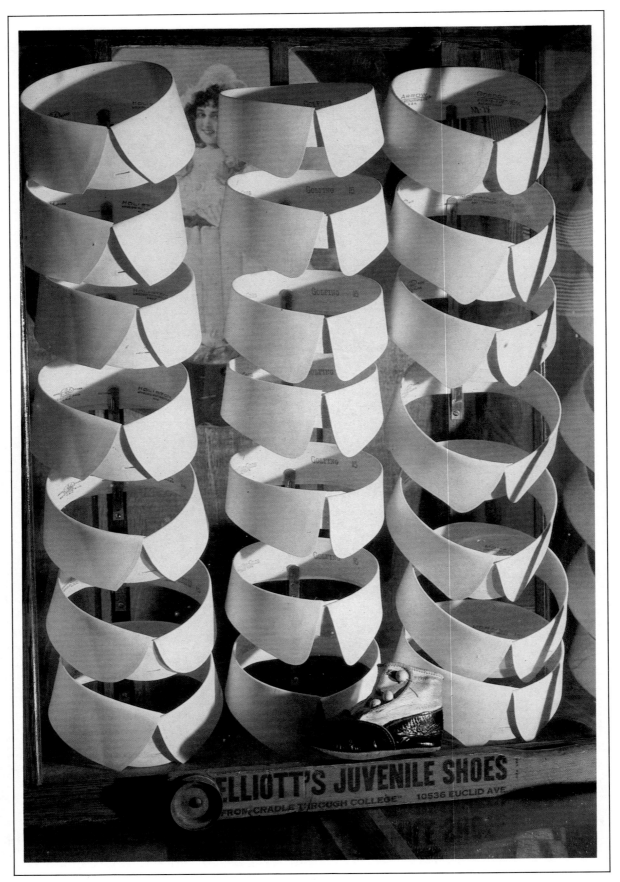

Oak display case for Arrow collars, c. early 1900's. Elliott's Juvenile Shoes "give away" to children for rolling iron barrel hoops.

Peter's Shoes display stand and two-tone button shoes, c. 1915.

Hat pins, c. 1900.

Oak counter with glass front, c. 1910.

Shelf price marker.

Spitting on the walls and floors was expressly prohibited by order of the State Board of Health. The Board did not limit a customer's right to expectorate on the ceiling.

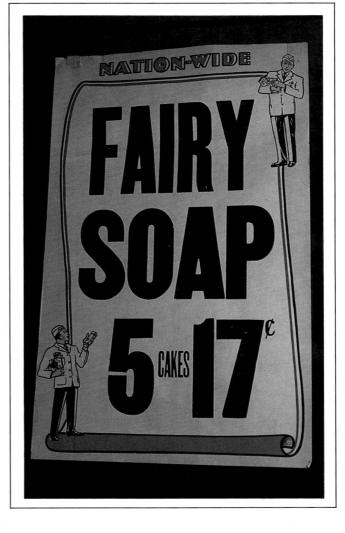

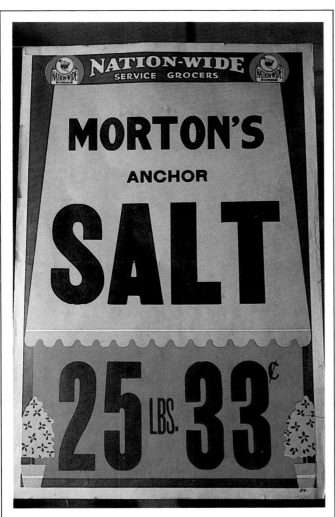

Nation-Wide grocer's broadside for "specials".

Many stores sold tools, clothing and household supplies in addition to groceries.

When locally owned stores gradually began to go out of business they were replaced by fast-emerging chain stores. It became a badge of pride for surviving stores to band together and display a sign that proclaimed they were not part of a chain operation.

Many stores in the 1920's served multiple purposes. They were post offices, pharmacies and Railway Express agencies.

"Drummers" encouraged store owners to promote their products by giving away samples of bread or canned goods with their purchases. After a customer had brought a predetermined dollar amount of goods he was given a coupon that could be redeemed on his next visit.

After the First World War many stores began to carry automobile supplies for the growing number of customers who had bought cars. Davis Tires were especially popular in the Midwest.

Tobacco Chronology

The variety of toabacco-related collectibles is staggering. Signs, boxes, broadsides, tin containers and store displays were produced by almost every firm.

1885-1900	The consumption of chewing tobacco reached its highest point with hundreds of brands offered to customers. Many were flavored with fruits, rum, honey, sugar or licorice
1905-1915	Cigars replaced chewing tobacco as the most favored product
Early 1920's	Cigarettes become the nation's most popular form of tobacco

Terms

"Plug" tobacco was pressed into cakes or twisted and designed to be chewed.

"Cut" plug tobacco was shredded so it could be "rolled" into cigarettes, chewed or used with a pipe.

"Lunchbox" tobacco containers were used during the first quarter of the twentieth century by manufacturers who felt their unique style would stimulate sales. A generation of children carried their lunches to rural schools in "lunchbox" tins after the tobacco was used.

Dating Tobacco Tins

Many tobacco companies bought tax stamps for their products and used them over a period as long as twenty years. This makes dating a particular tobacco tin precisely a difficult task. The tax stamp on the tin indicates that it was not used prior to the date on the stamp but it provides only a starting point.

Roly Poly Tobacco Containers

The "Roly Poly" tin was patented on November 5, 1912. The patent was issued to Washington Tuttle of Baltimore, Maryland. Four companies (Mayo, Dixie Queen, Red Indian, U.S. Marine) used the unusual containers for their tobacco. The Red Indian and U.S. Marine brands only issued the Satisfied Customer, the Dutchman and the Man from Scotland Yard (Inspector). Mayo and Dixie Queen added the Storekeeper, Singing Waiter and Mammy to the other three and offered sets of six.

Pocket Tins

Commonly Found	Rare
Tuxedo	Gold Dust
Prince Albert	Taxi
Half and Half	Scissors
Union Leader	Bull Dog
Velvet	Bambino
Revelation	Stanwix Ground Plug
Edgeworth	Salowitz
	Hindoo

Many times a slight variation in design can make a fairly common tobacco tin rare. The Honey Moon Tobacco pocket tin with a man smoking a pipe on the moon (one-on-the-moon) is fairly easily found. The variation shows a formally dressed couple on the same size moon. The "two-on-the-moon" is considered rare.

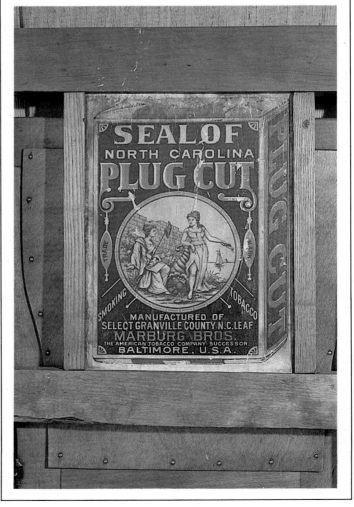

Seal of North Carolina Plug Cut folding chair, c. 1930's.

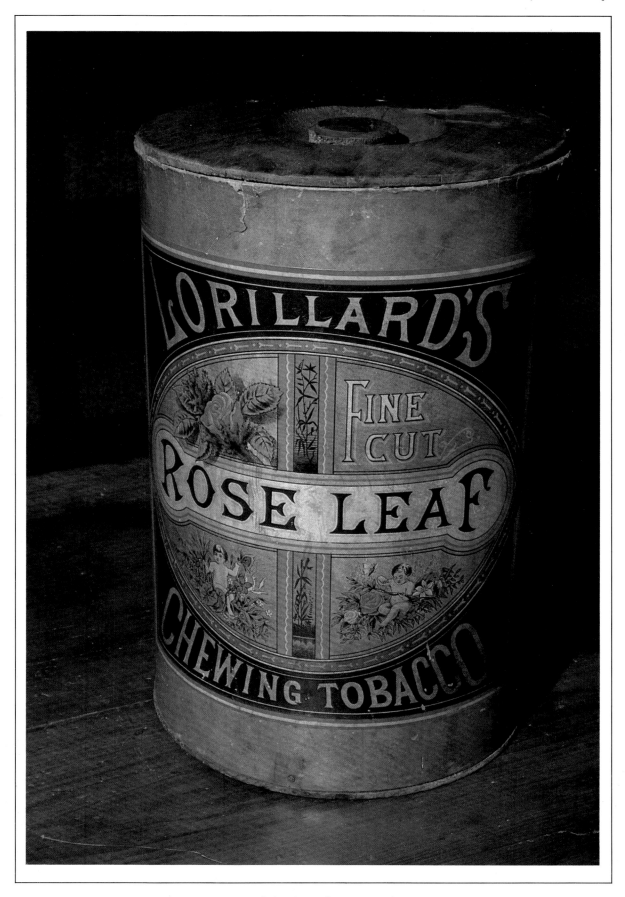

Rose Leaf chewing tobacco container.

Exterior Mail Pouch tobacco sign.

Cigar boxes.

Bank Note "stand-up" display.

War Eagle two for 5¢ cigar containers.

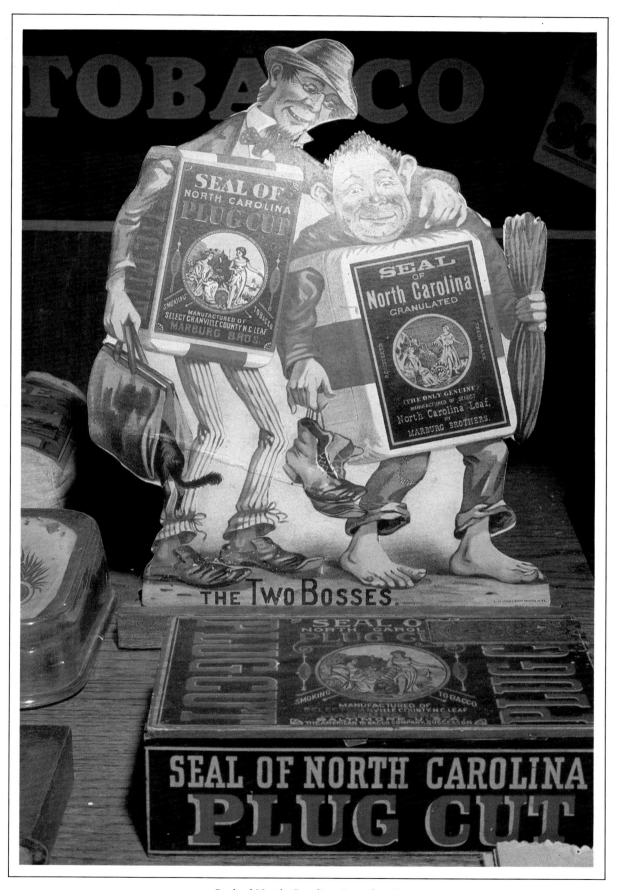

Seal of North Carolina "stand-up".

Variety of early twentieth century tobacco packages.

Old Honesty and
Plow Boy canvas banners.

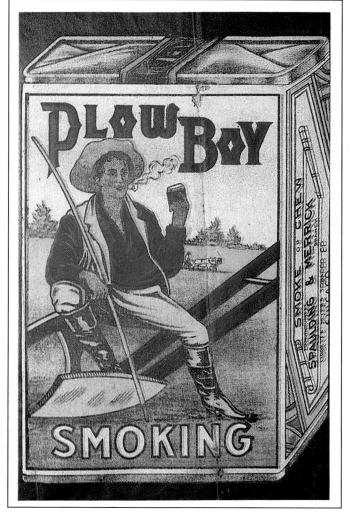

Greenback Tobacco paper sign, #4 in a set of four.

Greenback Smoking Tobacco.

Jars of Dill's Best and Stag tobacco.

Jar of Allen and Ginter's smoking tobacco.

"Round flat" of Ojibwa tobacco and three cans of Possum cigars.

Lucky Strike Roll Cut smoking tobacco in original unopened jar.

Flegner's Tobacco paper "stand-up", dated 1890.

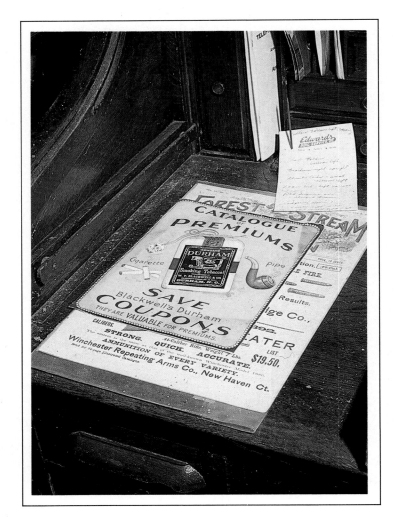

Catalog for ordering premiums with tobacco coupons.

Spaulding and Merrick tobacco container.

Box of Dill's Pipe Cleaners, metal Popper's Ace, and an unopened box of Peachey Chewing Tobacco.

Old Briar "stand-up" counter display.

Hambone 5¢ Cigar chalkboard.

Postmaster Cigar counter dispenser.

Red Coon Chewing Tobacco metal sign. In recent years this sign has been reproduced in significant quantities. This example is an original Red Coon sign from the 1930's.

Lucke's Telescopes were five for 10¢ in 1918.

A full box of Old Virginia Cheroots.

Packages of Old Virginia Cheroots.

Penny match dispenser, c. 1920's.

Ohio Blue Tip match dispenser, c. 1940's.

Lucky Strike clock, octagon "school house" form, c. 1910.

Counsellor Cigar sign.

Blue Moon cardboard box that contained individual packages of tobacco.

Right Cut dispenser for plug tobacco.

Union Leader, Sweet Cuba, Bachelor and Mechanics Delight offered a full line of tobacco products in the early 1900's.

The Seal of North Carolina "stand-up" sign dates from about 1910.

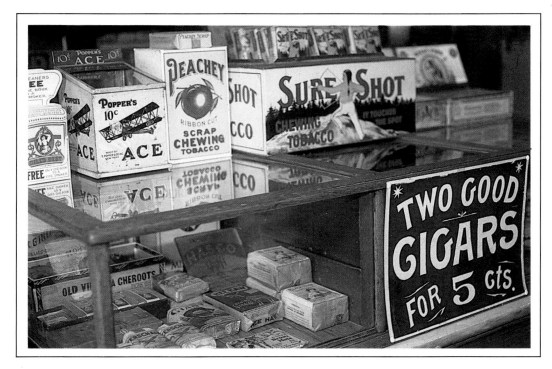

There were hundreds of brands of tobacco for chewing, rolling cigarettes and pipe smoking in the 1880-1920 period. Eventually many of the small independent brands were absorbed by much larger national tobacco corporations.

Variety of cigars in their original boxes.

Sweet Laurel Plug tobacco broom holder.

Cyclone cardboard sign.

Big John Plug Cut "stand-up."

Possum "3 for 10¢ Extra Mild, Extra Good" Cigars and Whale Tobacco.

Red Ranger Cigar box.

Metal Sure Shot chewing tobacco container and packages.

Sweet Cuba containers were made in several colors. Yellow is the most commonly found and blue is extremely rare.

Sweet Cuba tub or bucket of chewing tobacco.

Mallard Cut Plug from LaCrosse, Wisconsin.

Variety of chewing and pipe tobacco from the first quarter of the twentieth century.

The Dixie Kid Cut Plug is probably the rarest of the group.

Full box of Kipling flat pocket tins.

Union Leader containers are among the most commonly found.

Pinch Hit paper banner.

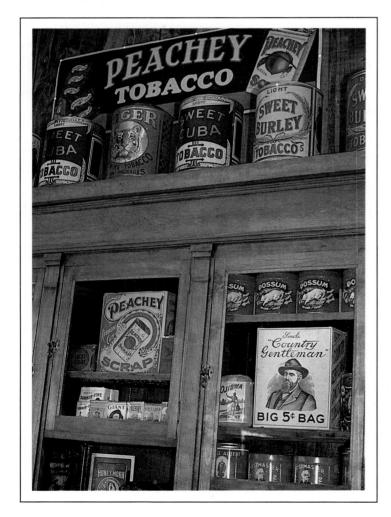

Peachey Tobacco canvas banner.

A product with a sports-related package generally has its value increased. Home Run cigarettes appear to be semi-valuable. Unfortunately, they are not old.

Jockey Top Little Cigars and Burley Cub Little Cigars, c. 1925.

Box of Yankee Girl Scrap tobacco and 20¢ size package.

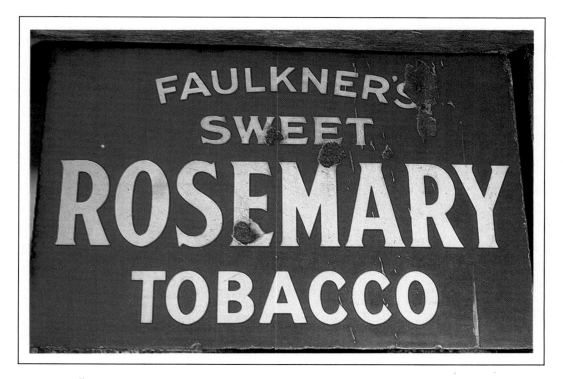

Faulkner's Sweet Rosemary Tobacco metal sign, English in origin, c. early 1900's.

Central Union Cut Plug "lunch box" container.

Stoneware vendor's jug made for Poland Mineral Springs Water Co. of Boston, c. 1870. A vendor's jug was specifically made for the company that has its name and address impressed into the neck of the jug. The pottery that produced the piece seldom put its mark on the stoneware.

Cushman and Company vendor's jug from Albany, New York, c. 1860's.

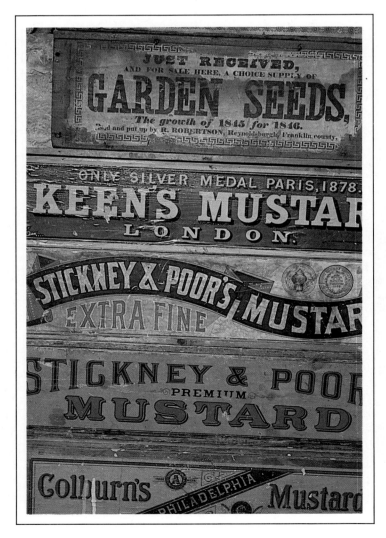

In recent years there has been an increased interest in the wide variety of product boxes that were manufactured in the 1880-1910 period. Spices, seeds, shoe polish and cinnamon were boxed and distributed to grocery stores. After the contents were sold the boxes were typically thrown away or used as kindling.

Nineteenth century grocery stores that could not afford to order factory-made oak shelving, counters and storage cabinets were forced to have their store fixtures locally made of pine and painted. In the 1880's many of the pine fixtures were grained to resemble oak.

Each drawer usually held a specific item with the contents stenciled on the drawer front.

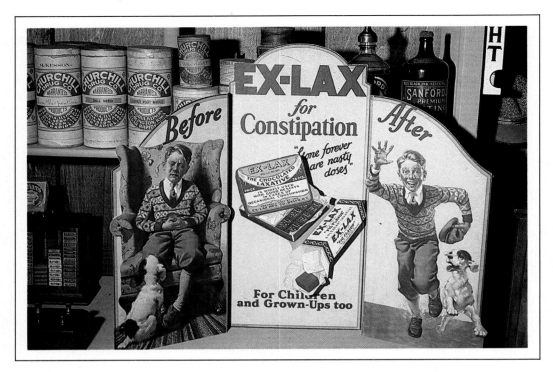

Ex-Lax "stand-up" sign from the 1930's.

Ayer's Sassaparilla cardboard "stand-up" from Lowell, Massachusetts, late nineteenth century.

Ayer's Pills "stand-up", headache pills, c. late nineteenth century.

Reverse sides of the Ayer's "stand-ups".

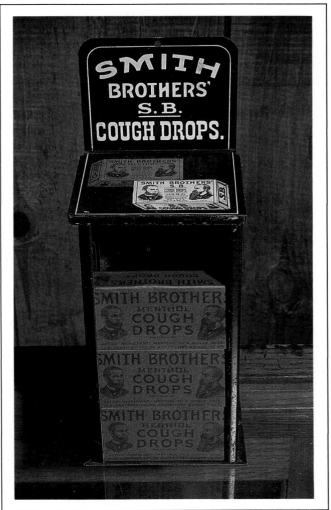

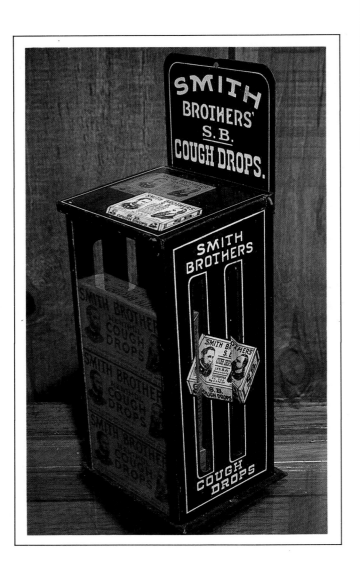

Smith Brothers Cough Drops dispenser.

Smith Brothers cough syrup.

Dr. Drake's Croup Remedy, c. 1900.

Larger version of Drake's Croup Remedy in a "stand-up".

Dr. J.H. McLean's canvas banner.

Variety of lice powders.

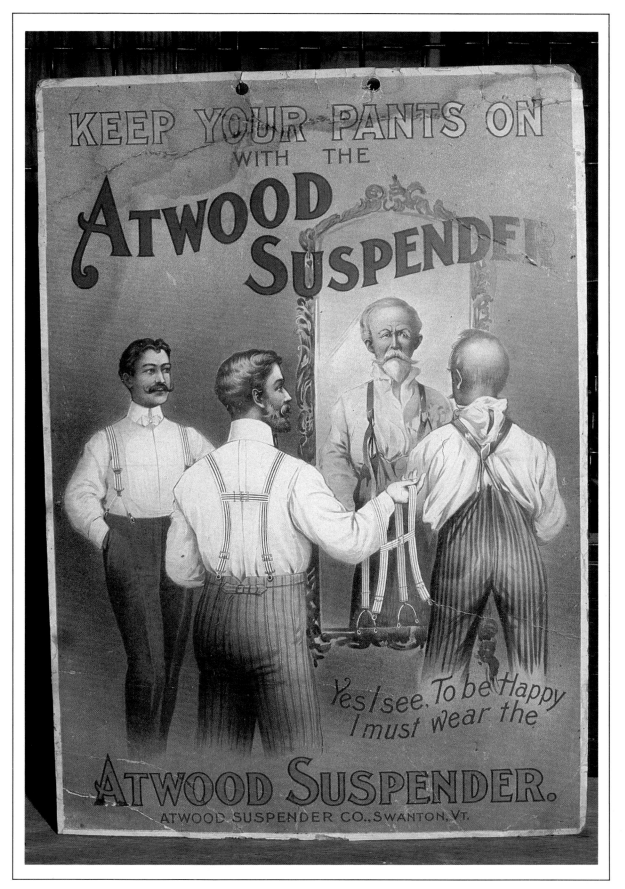

Atwood Suspender's sign.

Peters Weatherbird Shoes wooden sign that was placed on the floor of the store.

Betsy Ross Shoe Polish box and individual tins.

Brown Shoe Company advertising match holder.

Hosiery display.

Stevenson Underwear "stand-up".

Northrup, King and Company seed box, hinged lid, designed to be hung from the wall of the store, c. 1930.

Overside seed jacket or "paper" from W.D. Burt Company.

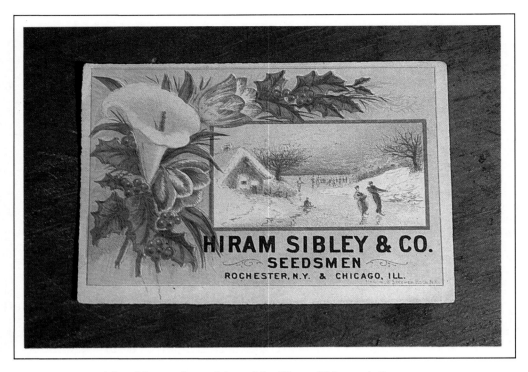

Advertising trade card issued by Hiram Sibley and Company.

Hiram Sibley seed box, c. 1885.

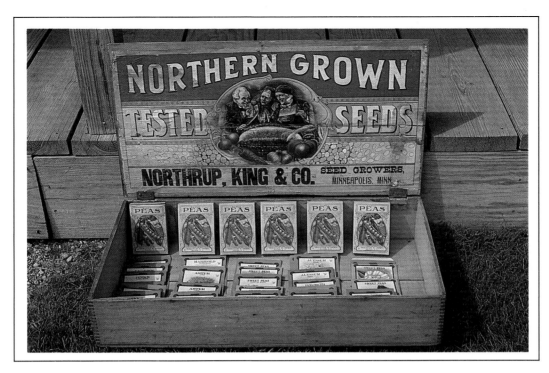

Northrup, King and Company counter seed box.

The Shakers were in the seed business at Mt. Lebanon, New York for almost a century. They are credited with being the first to sell goods on consignment. Grocery stores were provided with boxes filled with Shaker-grown seeds. When the seeds were sold the grocer kept one-third and returned the balance to the Shakers.

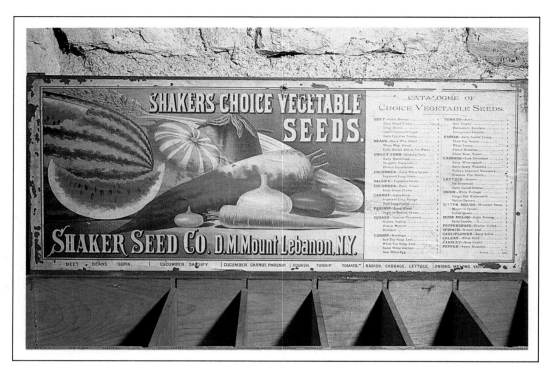

Seldom is a Shaker seed box found with a colorful interior label. This label is especially rare.

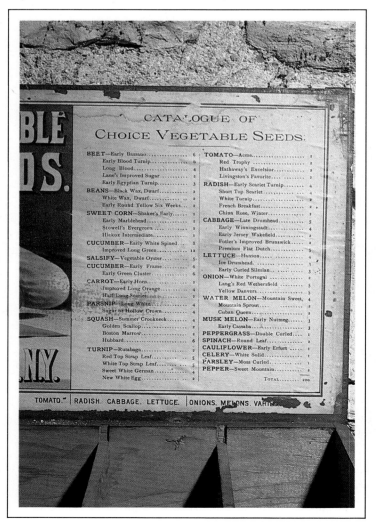

The variety of seeds that was available to gardeners in the late nineteenth century was staggering. Many varities listed on the interior label no longer exist.

Most seed boxes were made of poplar or pine and were not painted or stained. The boxes were usual-ly nailed together or held by factory-made dovetails. It is not unusual to find a series of labels glued one upon the other on the boxes.

Seed boxes from the 1890-1915 period tend to be made of oak and are considerably smaller in size than the earlier boxes. Briggs Brothers boxes are typical of many of the period.

These three seed boxes from the first decade of the twentieth century are fairly common.

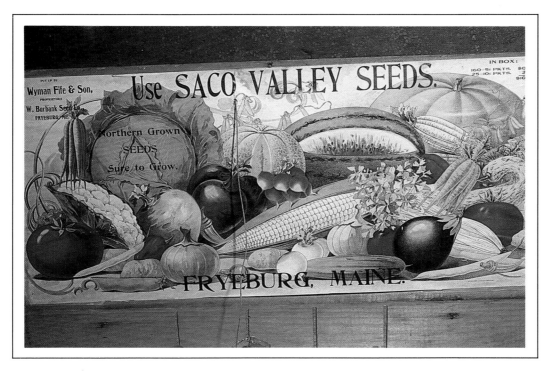

On occasion it was possible for two different seed companies to use the same graphic grouping of fruits and vegetables in their advertising. This interior label from a Maine company was also used by a company from Sabetha, Kansas.

Both boxes date from approximately 1880-1900.

Interior of Budd D. Hawkins seed box from Reading, Vermont.

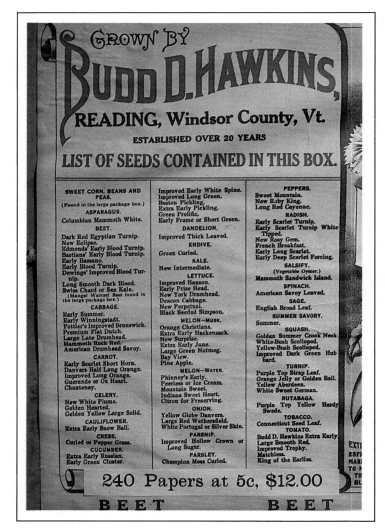

Hawkins offered an extensive variety of seeds at 5¢ per packet or "paper".

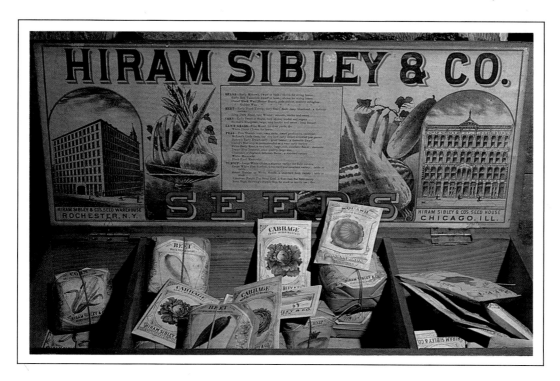

We had an opportunity to purchase this Sibley seed box near Lancaster, Pennsylvania. It was a surprise to find it filled with the original packets and bundles of seeds when the lid was opened.

Seeds from the Hiram Sibley & Co. box.

Ferry and Company watermelon and cabbage seeds in glass bottles. It is possible that these bottles were not supplied by Ferry but put together by an enterprising storeowner with the front of a packet cut out and glued to the bottle.

Price Guide

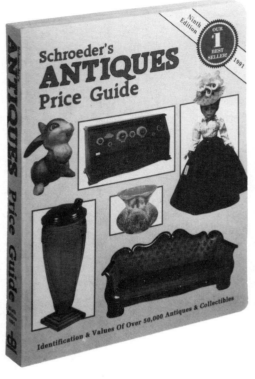